101 FACTS ABOUT CRISTIANO RONALDO THAT EVERY KID NEEDS TO KNOW!

Discover Fun Facts and Amazing Adventures of The World's Favorite Soccer Star

R. Parlour

WELCOME TO THE WORLD OF CR7!

Hey Ronaldo Fans! Are you ready to embark on an exciting adventure into the incredible world of Cristiano Ronaldo? This book is brimming with fun facts about your favorite football superstar that will make you admire him even more! Some of these details you might already know, but others will amaze and delight you.

Did you know Ronaldo began playing football as a little boy on the island of Madeira in Portugal? Or that he overcame a racing heart as a teen before becoming one of the greatest players ever? He also tackled early hurdles at Sporting Lisbon before joining the biggest clubs in the world. Ronaldo loves spending time with his family and keeps a huge collection of trophies in his museum. He was the first player ever to reach 100 goals in the UEFA Champions League. How impressive is that?

This book is filled with stories about Ronaldo's life, from his humble start to his incredible achievements, like winning five Ballon d'Or awards and leading Portugal to a European Championship. You'll see how his powerful shots, lightning-quick dribbles, and unshakable determination made him a global icon. You'll also learn about his big heart, as he often helps charities and inspires young players worldwide to believe in themselves.

So, grab your favorite snack, get cozy, and join us on this thrilling journey to learn all about Cristiano Ronaldo. Let's find out how many of these fun facts you already know and which ones will become your new favorites!

BONUS CHAPTER: WATCH RON'S MAGIC!

Are you ready to see Cristiano Ronaldo's incredible skills in action? **Scan the QR** code below to watch a special video of **Ronaldo's Top 10 Champions League Goals**! You'll witness powerful shots, jaw-dropping headers, and unforgettable moments that show why Ronaldo is a true football legend. Grab a tablet or smartphone, scan the code, and dive into the excitement of one of the greatest players in the history of the game. Get ready to cheer and be inspired by Ronaldo's amazing talents!

Enjoy the magic of Ronaldo and let his amazing goals inspire you to chase your own dreams!

1
A BOY FROM MADEIRA

Cristiano Ronaldo dos Santos Aveiro was born on February 5, 1985, on the Portuguese island of Madeira. Growing up in a humble neighborhood, he shared a small room with his siblings. Even as a little boy, he showed a huge passion for football, often kicking any ball-shaped object he could find.

2
NICKNAMED
"CRY-BABY"

When Ronaldo was young, his friends would sometimes call him "cry-baby." They joked that he would burst into tears whenever he or his team lost a match. Although that might sound funny, it also showed his fierce desire to win and his deep love for football. This competitive fire remained with him as he grew, and he learned to channel his emotions into training harder. In time, that passion and determination became strengths, leading him to push himself and others around him to always aim for victory.

3
LOVING A BALL SINCE AGE THREE

Ronaldo's earliest memories involve a football. At just three years old, he would spend hours every day kicking a ball around the narrow streets of Madeira. If he wasn't playing in the street, he was inside juggling or watching matches on television. His mother, Maria Dolores, has shared that even on rainy days, Cristiano would insist on going outside. This deep fascination with practicing his footwork and trying new tricks helped him develop the technical skills that would later amaze fans and opponents all over the world.

4
THE INFLUENCE OF HIS FATHER

Ronaldo's father introduced him to a more organized setting of the sport. Cristiano got to see how players trained, prepared their kits, and respected team rules. Watching those older players in a proper football environment encouraged him to dream bigger. Ronaldo has often mentioned that his father's involvement in football brought him closer to the game, setting the stage for the superstar he would become.

5
A SPECIAL MIDDLE NAME

Cristiano's middle name, "Ronaldo," was inspired by Ronald Reagan, the former President of the United States. His father admired Reagan for his strong public speaking skills. This is an unusual naming origin for a Portuguese child, making Cristiano's full name quite unique. Even so, Ronaldo himself has joked that he didn't have much say in it, but he appreciates having a name that stands out. Today, when people say "Ronaldo," most think of him before any other famous figure, proving how he's given the name global recognition.

6
EARLY STRUGGLES WITH EDUCATION

Ronaldo was so focused on football that his school life sometimes took a back seat. He once admitted that he wasn't very interested in formal education. In fact, he left school around age 14 to fully dedicate himself to football training. Although this choice was risky, especially for someone from a less privileged background, he believed wholeheartedly in his talent. With his mother's support, he followed his passion for the sport, determined to make a career out of it. Looking back, it's clear that his bet on himself paid off.

7
SIGNING WITH SPORTING LISBON

When Ronaldo was only 12 years old, Sporting Lisbon recognized his potential and signed him for a fee that was substantial for such a young player. Leaving his island home and moving to Lisbon was a huge change. It meant living in a dormitory away from his family for most of the year, training hard every day to polish his talent. Despite feeling homesick, he remained focused on improving his skills. Over time, he became one of Sporting's brightest youth prospects, catching the attention of Europe's top clubs.

8
RACING PAST TEAMMATES

During his time with Sporting Lisbon's youth academy, Ronaldo stood out by being extremely fast. His sprinting ability and agility stunned his peers. Coaches have shared stories of how he would run past opponents with ease, sometimes making them look like they were standing still. This speed, combined with his creative footwork, made him nearly impossible to catch. He worked tirelessly in the gym and on the pitch to grow stronger and faster. By age 15, many predicted he would become one of Portugal's best attacking players.

9
LIFE-CHANGING GROWTH SPURT

Around the age of 14 or 15, Ronaldo experienced a growth spurt that transformed him from a skinny boy into a taller, more muscular athlete. He gained a few inches in height relatively quickly, which helped him improve his heading ability and physical presence. Coaches noticed that his entire style changed after he learned to use his new body shape to shield the ball and power through defenders. This physical development, combined with his dedication to practice, gave him a clear advantage over other players in his age group.

10
1ST LISBON SENIOR APPEARANCE

Ronaldo's dream of playing professional football at the highest level came true on August 14, 2002. He debuted for Sporting Lisbon's senior team in the Primeira Liga, Portugal's top football division. Despite being only 17 years old, he showed confidence on the ball and dazzled fans with his footwork. Although he didn't score in that first match, he caught the eyes of scouts from across Europe. It was just the beginning of a career that would take him to some of the biggest clubs in the world.

11
FRIENDLY THAT CHANGED IT ALL

In August 2003, Sporting Lisbon hosted Manchester United for a friendly match to inaugurate Sporting's new stadium. Ronaldo put on an eye-catching performance, dribbling past defenders and creating opportunities. Manchester United's players were so impressed that they urged manager Sir Alex Ferguson to sign him immediately. Within days, the club secured his transfer, making Ronaldo the first Portuguese player to sign for Manchester United. This match is often remembered as the turning point that launched him into international stardom at a very young age.

12
A TEENAGE TRANSFER RECORD

Upon joining Manchester United in 2003, Ronaldo became the most expensive teenager in English football history at the time. The fee was around £12.24 million, a massive sum for an 18-year-old. This move generated excitement and skepticism alike, as many wondered if he could live up to such a price tag. Ronaldo, however, saw the fee as a testament to his potential and was determined to prove his worth. His success at Manchester United would later show that the investment was more than justified.

13
THE FAMOUS
NUMBER 7

When Ronaldo arrived at Manchester United, he initially asked for the number 28, the same he wore at Sporting Lisbon. However, Sir Alex Ferguson insisted he take the iconic number 7, previously worn by club legends like George Best, Eric Cantona, and David Beckham. Ronaldo felt immense pressure to live up to that legacy, but he embraced the challenge. Over time, he made the number 7 shirt his own, becoming synonymous with that jersey worldwide. This tradition of excellence motivated him to push his game to new heights.

14
DEBUT FOR
UNITED

Ronaldo made his debut for Manchester United on August 16, 2003, against Bolton Wanderers. Though he started on the bench, he came on as a substitute in the second half. Immediately, fans saw flashes of brilliance: step-overs, quick sprints, and explosive creativity. The crowd at Old Trafford gave him a standing ovation at the end, recognizing they'd just witnessed something special. He didn't score that day, but his presence felt electric, setting the tone for a career filled with memorable moments for the Red Devils.

15
FIRST TROPHY AT OLD TRAFFORD

Ronaldo's first major trophy with Manchester United came in the 2003–2004 season when the team won the FA Cup. In the final, Ronaldo scored the opening goal against Millwall, showcasing his flair on a big stage. Winning silverware so early in his Premier League career boosted his confidence and endeared him to United supporters. It also hinted at the winning mentality he would carry throughout his career. Collecting trophies soon became a habit for him, and this FA Cup victory was the first of many.

16
PERSONAL TRAGEDY AND STRENGTH

In January 2005, Ronaldo faced a personal hardship when his father's health deteriorated due to alcoholism. Despite the emotional weight, he continued performing for Manchester United, using football as an escape. Sadly, his father passed away in September 2005. Ronaldo was deeply affected, but he honored his father's memory by dedicating his performances to him. This emotional period shaped Ronaldo, driving him to achieve greater heights. The support from teammates and fans helped him cope, and he emerged stronger, carrying his father's spirit in his heart.

17
BUILDING A FINELY TUNED BODY

While at Manchester United, Ronaldo became known for his strict training routines and disciplined diet. He added muscle through intense gym sessions, focusing on strength, speed, and agility. He practiced sprint drills, plyometrics, and flexibility exercises, which helped him master quick changes of direction on the pitch. Teammates were often amazed by how serious he was about physical conditioning, even arriving early and staying late to work on his physique. This approach turned him into a robust, explosive athlete who could out-jump, out-sprint, and outlast many opponents.

18
FIRST PREMIER LEAGUE TITLE

Ronaldo won his first Premier League title with Manchester United in the 2006–2007 season. This triumph was significant because it ended Chelsea's dominance and showcased Ronaldo's growing influence on the team's success. He contributed key goals and assists, gradually becoming one of the league's top performers. The title also marked the beginning of a new era at Old Trafford, where Ronaldo, alongside other talented teammates, formed a fearsome attacking lineup. Winning this trophy set the stage for his eventual recognition as one of the world's best players.

19
FIFA WORLD PLAYER NOMINATION

By 2007, Ronaldo's performances earned him a nomination for the FIFA World Player of the Year award. While he didn't win that year, his name appeared alongside legends like Kaká and Lionel Messi. This nomination proved that he'd made the leap from a promising young talent to a global star. Fans across continents started paying more attention to his dribbling skills, powerful shots, and signature free-kicks. Though the award eluded him that season, it signaled the start of numerous accolades that would come his way.

20
DOMINATING THE PREMIER LEAGUE

The 2007–2008 season was a breakthrough for Ronaldo. He scored 31 Premier League goals, earning the Golden Boot and the Premier League Player of the Season award. His blend of speed, skill, and clinical finishing made him nearly unplayable. Opposing defenders struggled to contain his tricks and direct running. Manchester United also clinched the league title again, and fans worldwide recognized Ronaldo as a footballing phenomenon. This season was vital for shaping his confidence and reputation, proving he was ready to compete with the best on any stage.

21
STUNNING GOAL AGAINST PORTO

In the 2008–2009 UEFA Champions League quarterfinal, Ronaldo scored a jaw-dropping long-range strike against FC Porto. The ball traveled about 40 yards before rocketing into the net. The goal not only secured victory for Manchester United but also earned him the FIFA Puskás Award for the best goal of the year. Commentators and fans hailed it as one of the most spectacular strikes they'd ever seen. This ability to score from incredible distances became a defining characteristic of Ronaldo's style, leaving defenders and goalkeepers helpless.

22
FIRST BALLON D'OR TRIUMPH

In 2008, Ronaldo crowned his outstanding year by winning his first Ballon d'Or, an award given annually to the best player in the world. His exceptional performances with Manchester United, including winning the Premier League and the UEFA Champions League, solidified his claim. He beat out Lionel Messi and Fernando Torres for the honor. This recognition placed him among an elite group of footballers. For a boy from Madeira who once cried over losing street matches, becoming the world's best was a dream realized. It marked the beginning of a legendary rivalry with Messi.

23
DRAMATIC MOVE TO REAL MADRID

In June 2009, Real Madrid purchased Ronaldo from Manchester United for a then-world-record fee of £80 million. Many considered it the biggest transfer story of the decade. Ronaldo had often expressed admiration for Real Madrid, and Los Blancos fans were delighted to welcome him. He inherited the number 9 jersey initially, later reclaiming the number 7. This transfer brought him to the Santiago Bernabéu, where he aimed to continue dominating football. The move also set the stage for epic showdowns in Spain's La Liga, particularly against FC Barcelona.

24
IMPACT AT THE BERNABÉU

Ronaldo wasted no time proving his worth at Real Madrid. He scored in each of his first four La Liga matches, breaking a club record for the best scoring start in the league. Fans quickly embraced him, chanting his name at the Bernabéu. Although Real Madrid faced strong competition from Barcelona during those years, Ronaldo's remarkable goal-scoring rate revitalized the club's spirit. His rivalry with Lionel Messi intensified during this period, creating some of the most memorable El Clásico matches in history.

25
FRIENDSHIP WITH MARCELO

During his time at Real Madrid, Ronaldo developed a close friendship with Brazilian left-back Marcelo. The two were often seen joking around in training sessions, doing goal celebrations together, and posting fun pictures on social media. Their bond was also evident on the pitch, where Marcelo's overlapping runs and Ronaldo's positioning created deadly attacking opportunities. The pair's camaraderie symbolized the strong team spirit that helped Real Madrid secure multiple titles. Even after Ronaldo left the club, they remained good friends, showcasing Ronaldo's ability to form lasting connections.

26
"DIVING" CRITICISM

Early in his career, Ronaldo sometimes faced criticism for going down easily during tackles, leading opponents and pundits to accuse him of "diving." Such accusations followed him particularly in the Premier League, where physical play is common. Determined to prove his critics wrong, he focused on strengthening his balance and reducing complaints by staying on his feet more often. Over time, he developed a stronger reputation for resilience. Though the accusations still surfaced occasionally, Ronaldo's actual skill and performance ultimately overshadowed any lingering criticism about this aspect of his game.

27
Becoming "CR7"

Although Ronaldo wore different jersey numbers early on, the iconic "CR7" brand emerged at Manchester United, where he donned the famous number 7. Embracing this nickname, he expanded it into a personal brand, launching CR7 clothing lines, fragrances, and leisurewear. Over time, "CR7" became synonymous with his style and excellence both on and off the pitch. He turned the brand into a global phenomenon, reflecting his commitment to perfection and innovation. Today, many football fans worldwide recognize "CR7" instantly, showing how marketing savvy and athletic success can go hand in hand.

28
A MASTER OF FREE-KICKS

One of the most memorable aspects of Ronaldo's skill set is his unique free-kick technique. He positions the ball carefully, steps back a few paces, and strikes it with the top of his foot to produce a powerful, often unpredictable trajectory. Over his career, he has scored numerous free-kick goals that left goalkeepers puzzled. Coaches and teammates have marveled at his dedication to practicing the craft, sometimes spending extra hours on the training ground. That commitment paid off, transforming him into one of the most feared set-piece specialists in world football.

29
A POWERHOUSE IN THE AIR

Ronaldo's ability to head the ball is legendary. With an impressive vertical leap that rivals basketball players, he often towers above defenders to score crucial goals. Whether it's a thunderous header from a corner or a precise flick-on from a cross, Ronaldo's timing and positioning are impeccable. He strengthened his neck muscles and honed his jumping technique during extra gym sessions, turning a once-average aerial game into a lethal weapon. Spectators regularly witness him hang in mid-air, waiting to direct the ball into the net with unstoppable force.

30
THREE PREMIER LEAGUE TITLES

During his time at Manchester United from 2003 to 2009, Ronaldo helped the club win three Premier League titles. The trio of victories came in consecutive seasons: 2006–2007, 2007–2008, and 2008–2009. Each season, he contributed essential goals and assists, forming a lethal partnership with teammates like Wayne Rooney. These triumphs cemented United's dominance in English football and showcased Ronaldo's evolution from a flashy trickster to a complete attacking force. His Premier League success laid the foundation for further accomplishments on a global stage and turned him into an Old Trafford legend.

31
FIRST CHAMPIONS LEAGUE TRIUMPH

In the 2007–2008 season, Ronaldo tasted continental glory by winning the UEFA Champions League with Manchester United. They faced Chelsea in the final, where Ronaldo opened the scoring with a powerful header. The match ended in a penalty shootout, and although Ronaldo missed his spot-kick, the team still emerged victorious. This triumph was a major milestone in his career, fulfilling a long-held dream of lifting Europe's most prestigious club trophy. It also boosted his confidence, reinforcing the idea that hard work and belief can bring the highest accolades in football.

32
HIGHEST SCORING SEASON

In the 2011–2012 La Liga season, Ronaldo reached a personal milestone by scoring an astonishing 46 league goals for Real Madrid. Coupled with other competitions, he ended the season with a tally surpassing 60 in all tournaments. This scoring spree helped Real Madrid clinch the title over arch-rivals Barcelona, signaling a shift in the power balance of Spanish football. His prolific form astounded fans and pundits alike, and it further cemented his rivalry with Lionel Messi, who also racked up huge numbers. It remains one of Ronaldo's standout achievements at the Bernabéu.

33
EURO 2012
HEARTBREAK

Ronaldo led Portugal into Euro 2012, hoping to guide his nation to European glory. Although Portugal reached the semifinals, they lost to Spain on penalties. Ronaldo had a strong tournament, scoring memorable goals and carrying much of the attacking burden. Fans and teammates admired his determination and leadership. Despite the heartbreak, he used the experience to grow stronger, understanding that international success required unity and relentless effort. This lesson would prove invaluable in the years ahead when he would finally lift a major trophy with his country.

34
THE FAMOUS VOLCANO RUN

In 2010, due to the Icelandic volcano eruption that disrupted flights, Real Madrid traveled by bus and train to face Olympique Lyon in a Champions League match. The journey took more than a day, a stark contrast to the usual quick flights. Ronaldo used this bizarre situation to bond with teammates, chatting, joking, and keeping spirits high. Though the journey was exhausting, his commitment to professionalism never wavered. It's a story many Real Madrid fans recall fondly, illustrating how Ronaldo adapted to challenges without letting them affect his performance.

35
GENEROUS
PHILANTHROPIST

Ronaldo is known for his charitable acts off the pitch. He's donated large sums of money to hospitals, disaster relief efforts, and various children's charities. One notable act was paying for a child's brain surgery, ensuring the family wouldn't face financial hardship. Another example is auctioning off personal awards or memorabilia to raise funds for worthy causes. He's also been named a "Save the Children" ambassador. These gestures show that behind the flashy goals and glamorous lifestyle lies a compassionate individual who believes in giving back to those in need.

36
FIFA BALLON D'OR 2013

After losing the Ballon d'Or to Lionel Messi in four consecutive years, Ronaldo finally reclaimed the prestigious award in 2013. Despite Barcelona's domestic success, Ronaldo's personal statistics and influence on Real Madrid were impossible to ignore. During an emotional acceptance speech, tears welled up as he thanked his family and teammates. It was a testament to his perseverance, proving that continuous hard work and resilience could overcome even the toughest competition. This win reignited the Messi-Ronaldo debate, making the rivalry even more thrilling for football fans worldwide.

37
"RONALDO CHOP"

One of Ronaldo's signature moves is the "Ronaldo Chop," a dribbling trick where he flicks the ball behind his standing leg while moving quickly. This sudden change in direction often bamboozles defenders. He started popularizing this move during his Manchester United days and continued perfecting it in Spain. Many young players try to imitate it on school playgrounds and local pitches, hoping to surprise opponents. The chop adds flair to his game, demonstrating his creativity and confidence on the ball. It remains a staple in his arsenal of deadly dribbling skills.

38
CLASH WITH MOURINHO

During his time at Real Madrid, Ronaldo played under manager José Mourinho, another Portuguese icon. Although they share a nationality, they occasionally clashed over tactics and personalities. Mourinho once criticized Ronaldo's work rate in certain matches, while Ronaldo felt he knew best how to approach his game. Despite these disagreements, they won La Liga and other trophies together, proving that even conflicting viewpoints can lead to success. Over time, both men expressed mutual respect in interviews, acknowledging that their differences stemmed from a burning desire to win.

39
BLOOD DONOR

Ronaldo has consistently advocated for blood donation and is known to donate blood himself regularly. He avoids having tattoos specifically to comply with medical guidelines for donors. He has joined campaigns urging fans to become donors, highlighting the importance of saving lives. This selflessness encourages others to think about how simple acts can create a big impact. By lending his global fame to such a worthy cause, Ronaldo shows that being a football star isn't just about scoring goals but also about using influence to make the world a better place.

40
61 GOAL SEASON

The 2014–2015 season saw Ronaldo hit another remarkable milestone, scoring 61 goals in all competitions for Real Madrid. This included 48 in La Liga, the most he'd ever netted in a single league campaign. He reached these numbers through relentless finishing, scoring with both feet and his head. Critics who once questioned his consistency were silenced. Although Real Madrid didn't clinch the league title that season, Ronaldo's personal achievements underscored his ability to keep improving. He defied assumptions that a forward must slow down or score less as he ages.

41
EURO 2016 TRIUMPH

One of Ronaldo's proudest moments came when Portugal won Euro 2016. Despite being injured early in the final against France, Ronaldo cheered his teammates from the sidelines, acting almost like a second coach. He delivered motivational words and urged them to push through fatigue. Thanks to Éder's winning goal, Portugal lifted the trophy for the first time in their history. Although Ronaldo couldn't fully participate on the pitch after his injury, his leadership and influence were undeniable. It was the international title he'd chased since his youth, finally achieved.

42
"SIIII" CELEBRATION

Ronaldo's trademark "Siiii" celebration is recognized worldwide. After scoring, he often leaps, spins in mid-air, and shouts "Siiii," meaning "Yes!" in Spanish. Fans in stadiums chant along, creating an electric atmosphere. Initially, this celebration developed spontaneously, but it quickly became a signature move. Media outlets use it as an iconic reference whenever he hits the back of the net. This simple yet powerful act unites supporters, teammates, and the player himself in a moment of shared excitement, reflecting the passion and joy Ronaldo brings to football.

43
UCL SUCCESS AT REAL MADRID

Ronaldo's time at Real Madrid included four UEFA Champions League titles: 2014, 2016, 2017, and 2018. He played vital roles in each campaign, scoring in finals and leading the competition's goal charts. The team's "La Décima" triumph in 2014 broke a 12-year Champions League drought. Fans hailed him as "Mr. Champions League" for his consistent scoring, especially in knockout rounds. Each trophy underlined his knack for performing on the biggest stage. By 2018, Ronaldo had set numerous UCL records, making him arguably one of the greatest players in the tournament's history.

44
RETURN TO OLD TRAFFORD

Ronaldo returned to face Manchester United in the UEFA Champions League with Real Madrid in 2013. He received a warm welcome from Old Trafford fans who remembered his incredible performances for the Red Devils. Though he scored the deciding goal, he chose not to celebrate, out of respect for the club that shaped him. This mutual admiration continued when he later rejoined Manchester United in 2021. Even after moving again, the bond between Ronaldo and United remains unique, showing how his ties to the club run deeper than just professional terms.

45
OVERHEAD KICK AGAINST JUVENTUS

In the 2017–2018 Champions League quarterfinal, Ronaldo scored an unforgettable overhead kick against Juventus, considered one of the greatest goals in UCL history. Rising nearly head-high, he volleyed the ball into the net in mid-air, leaving fans from both teams in awe. Juventus supporters stood and applauded, a rare gesture of respect for an opposing player. This moment epitomized Ronaldo's athletic ability, focus, and showmanship. Later that summer, ironically, he transferred to Juventus, joining the club whose fans had honored his incredible skill just months earlier.

46
BLOCKBUSTER MOVE TO JUVENTUS

In July 2018, Ronaldo joined Juventus for a fee of around €100 million, shocking many as Real Madrid seemed inseparable from their star. He settled into the Italian Serie A quickly, scoring goals and helping Juventus maintain their domestic dominance. The club's fans grew to love his dedication and the professional attitude he brought to training. Although Juventus hoped to lift the Champions League trophy with him, they fell short each season. Still, his presence boosted Serie A's global viewership and emphasized that Ronaldo could excel in multiple leagues.

47
BREAKING THE 700-GOAL MARK

In October 2019, Ronaldo reached a personal milestone by scoring his 700th career goal for club and country. This statistic placed him among an elite few in football history. Demonstrating consistent excellence over many seasons, he netted this landmark goal during Portugal's Euro 2020 qualifying campaign. Critics who doubted he could keep up his pace past age 30 were once again proven wrong. Each goal carried a story of hard work, from intense training sessions to endless hours honing his technique. Surpassing 700 cemented his status as a modern legend.

48
COPPA ITALIA GLORY

In May 2021, Ronaldo won the Coppa Italia with Juventus, adding another significant trophy to his collection. Defeating Atalanta 2–1 in the final, Juventus lifted the trophy after a challenging season. Ronaldo played a key role throughout the tournament, scoring pivotal goals and assisting teammates. Although the team's league performance didn't match expectations that year, this victory showcased Ronaldo's knack for delivering silverware wherever he goes. He celebrated joyfully with fans and teammates, reinforcing his reputation as a guaranteed source of success for clubs aiming for trophies.

49
EMOTIONAL RETURN
TO UNITED

In August 2021, Ronaldo surprised the football world by returning to Manchester United after 12 years away. Fans welcomed him with open arms, filling social media with excited posts. The club store sold out of jerseys with his name almost instantly. Returning to Old Trafford felt like coming home, and he scored twice on his second debut against Newcastle. Although the team faced challenges in the Premier League, Ronaldo's presence brought renewed optimism. This move proved that even in his mid-30s, he remained determined to compete at the highest level.

50
MOVE TO
SAUDI ARABIA

At the end of 2022, Ronaldo made headlines by signing with Al Nassr in Saudi Arabia. The transfer shocked many, as he left European football after nearly two decades of dominating the biggest leagues. In Saudi Arabia, he joined a growing trend of global stars helping develop the region's football culture. Fans flocked to see him live, boosting Al Nassr's profile. Some critics questioned the move, but Ronaldo viewed it as a new challenge—proving his adaptability and commitment to promoting the sport on a worldwide scale.

51
CAPTAIN FANTASTIC
FOR PORTUGAL

Ronaldo first captained the Portuguese national team in 2007, stepping in as a leader both on and off the pitch. His teammates say he brings energy, motivation, and high expectations to the squad. Over the years, he's guided Portugal through major tournaments, encouraging younger players to believe in themselves. Even when injured or on the bench, he's known to rally the team, pacing the sidelines and offering advice. He proudly wears the captain's armband, seeing it as an honor and a responsibility to unite the players under one shared goal: victory.

52
THE INTERNATIONAL GOAL RECORD

In September 2021, Ronaldo officially became the men's all-time top scorer in international football, surpassing Ali Daei's long-standing record. Scoring his 110th and 111th Portugal goals against the Republic of Ireland etched his name even deeper into history. He continued adding to that tally in subsequent matches, proving age is just a number. Breaking this record highlighted his consistency and relentless pursuit of excellence. Even as he switched clubs and leagues, his commitment to his country never wavered, and each goal for Portugal further cemented his legendary status in world football.

53
RONALDO'S LOVE FOR MUSIC

Outside of football, Ronaldo enjoys listening to music—particularly pop and Latin tunes. He's shared playlists that include artists from Portugal, Spain, and beyond. Some days, he opts for upbeat songs that energize him before training, while other times he prefers calmer tracks to relax after intense matches. Teammates joke that he sometimes dances in the locker room, bringing a fun vibe to the squad. This love for music shows a lighter side to the intense athlete, reminding everyone that even global superstars benefit from letting loose and enjoying a good beat.

54
THE "CR7 SELFIE" PHENOMENON

Over the past decade, Ronaldo has embraced social media, often sharing selfies before and after matches. He's one of the most followed athletes on platforms like Instagram, where millions of fans eagerly await his posts. The famous "CR7 selfie" often features him smiling or celebrating a goal, giving supporters a behind-the-scenes peek at his daily life. He sometimes tags teammates, family members, or sponsors, showcasing his professional and personal relationships. By connecting directly with fans worldwide, Ronaldo bridges the gap between superstar and supporter, creating a sense of shared celebration.

55
FIRST PLAYER TO WIN THE BIG THREE

In 2019, Ronaldo achieved a remarkable feat by becoming the first player ever to win league titles in England (Premier League), Spain (La Liga), and Italy (Serie A). This trifecta highlights his adaptability and success in three of the most competitive leagues on the planet. Many players struggle when moving to a new country, coping with unfamiliar cultures and playing styles, but Ronaldo thrived. Each triumph underscored his commitment, drive, and talent. This record demonstrates that no matter where he goes, he finds a way to lead his team to victory.

56
EPIC RIVALRY WITH Lionel Messi

Few rivalries in sports match the intensity and mutual respect shared by Cristiano Ronaldo and Lionel Messi. For over a decade, they dominated individual awards, traded top scorer accolades, and pushed each other to higher levels. While fans often debate who's superior, both players have repeatedly praised one another. Their frequent El Clásico clashes for Real Madrid and Barcelona became legendary, capturing global attention. Each saw the other's performances and raised the bar, resulting in a golden era of modern football. This rivalry, built on skill and ambition, continues to fascinate enthusiasts worldwide.

57
TEAM OF MEDICAL EXPERTS

Ronaldo employs a personal fitness team that includes a nutritionist, physiotherapist, and personal trainer. Their goal is to keep him at peak physical condition year-round. He's famous for undergoing regular tests to measure body fat, muscle mass, and recovery times, adjusting workouts accordingly. This scientific approach means that even if he faces a small injury or muscle strain, his experts step in to help him bounce back quickly. With so many matches in a season, this level of care has allowed him to stay competitive at an age when many players slow down.

58
HEART RATE TRAINING SESSIONS

One of Ronaldo's training secrets is monitoring his heart rate during drills. He uses specialized trackers that show how hard he's working in real-time. When he notices his heart rate is too low, he ups the intensity. If it's too high, he takes a brief pause to prevent overexertion. This method helps him optimize his sprints, dribbles, and overall cardiovascular performance. Trainers have reported that Ronaldo aims to maintain excellent stamina, allowing him to make explosive runs in the final minutes of a match. This focus on fine-tuning every detail sets him apart.

59
DESIGNING HIS OWN HOTEL CHAIN

Partnering with the Pestana Hotel Group, Ronaldo launched "Pestana CR7" hotels in locations like Funchal (in Madeira), Lisbon, and Madrid. These hotels blend modern design with CR7-themed décor. Guests can find memorabilia, quotes, and references to Ronaldo's achievements throughout the lobbies and rooms. He's involved in the branding and overall concept, ensuring the properties reflect his style: sleek, energetic, and welcoming. This venture shows how Ronaldo has expanded beyond football, using his fame and eye for detail to create memorable experiences for traveling fans and tourists alike.

60
CR7 MUSEUM
IN MADEIRA

In Funchal, Ronaldo's hometown on Madeira Island, there's a museum dedicated to his life and achievements: the CR7 Museum. It houses trophies, medals, jerseys, and personal items from his childhood to his professional peak. Visitors can explore interactive exhibits, watch highlight reels of his best goals, and learn about pivotal moments in his career. A life-sized statue of Ronaldo stands outside, attracting fans who snap photos in admiration. The museum not only celebrates his successes but also inspires local kids, showing that someone from a small island can achieve global fame through dedication.

61
THE "ANKLE WEIGHTS" TRICK

Ronaldo reportedly uses ankle weights during some training drills to increase resistance. By adding extra weight, each movement—like quick turns or leaps—becomes more challenging. When he removes the weights, he feels lighter and can move faster. This trick aims to enhance agility and explosiveness, allowing him to beat defenders or adjust to sudden changes in match tempo. Coaches have noted that while ankle weights aren't used every day, they're part of a varied approach to training that keeps Ronaldo's body guessing and continuously improving.

62
LOVE FOR FAST CARS

Ronaldo has a well-known passion for luxury and sports cars. His collection includes brands like Bugatti, Ferrari, Lamborghini, and McLaren, often in limited-edition models. He occasionally shares pictures of new cars on social media, generating excitement among fans who admire both his success and his taste in high-performance vehicles. However, he also drives carefully, aware that any recklessness could risk his football career. Each car is a reward for his hard work, reflecting his belief that celebrating success can motivate him to achieve even more on the field.

63
COVID-19 HELP

In 2020, when the COVID-19 pandemic hit, Ronaldo and his agent, Jorge Mendes, donated essential medical equipment to Portuguese hospitals. They funded critical care units, ventilators, and other supplies to aid in the fight against the virus. This gesture relieved overwhelmed healthcare systems and saved lives in his homeland. Ronaldo also used his social media to encourage fans to follow safety guidelines and stay healthy. His involvement underscores that he views his platform as a tool for greater good, stepping up in times of global crisis to help communities in need.

64
FOCUS ON FAMILY

Ronaldo is a proud father of several children, including Cristiano Jr., twins Eva Maria and Mateo, and daughters Alana Martina and Bella Esmeralda. He frequently shares family photos, showing them celebrating birthdays, traveling, or cheering at matches. Despite his busy schedule, he prioritizes time with them, whether it's playing in the backyard or attending school events. Ronaldo has said being a father changes his perspective, teaching him responsibility and love in new ways. His partner, Georgina Rodríguez, also plays a big role, supporting the family's bond while he pursues football success.

65
BACALHAU À BRÁS

Although Ronaldo sticks to a strict, healthy diet, he occasionally treats himself to a traditional Portuguese dish called Bacalhau à Brás, made with salted cod, onions, eggs, and olives. It's a comfort food that reminds him of his roots in Madeira. His diet usually focuses on grilled fish, chicken, whole grains, and fresh fruits, but he's always happy to enjoy his country's famous delicacies in moderation. This balance between discipline and a taste of home helps keep him happy and ensures he stays connected to his cultural background.

66
Generous Tips

There are stories of Ronaldo leaving large tips at restaurants or hotels where he's had excellent service. On vacation in Greece after Portugal's Euro 2018 campaign, he reportedly left a hotel staff an especially generous tip to thank them for their hospitality. Such acts highlight his willingness to reward kindness and effort, no matter a person's profession. He once said he respects anyone who works hard and wants to make others happy, and leaving a generous tip is his way of expressing gratitude for good service.

67
THE IMPORTANCE OF SLEEP

Ronaldo is known to take sleep very seriously, understanding it's crucial for muscle recovery. He reportedly sleeps five times a day in shorter "naps" rather than a single long rest at night. By scheduling these naps after training sessions or matches, he ensures his body can repair more efficiently. Specialists have praised this method for high-performance athletes, saying it helps maintain optimal energy levels throughout the day. Ronaldo's approach to sleep stands out as just another example of how he leaves no stone unturned in pursuit of peak physical condition.

68
CHECKUPS WITH NUTRITIONISTS

Visiting a nutritionist regularly, Ronaldo tailors his meals to match his training schedule and matchday demands. His diet typically includes lean proteins like chicken or fish, whole-grain carbs, and plenty of vegetables. Cheat meals are rare but allowed occasionally—often traditional Portuguese dishes that remind him of home. He also drinks plenty of water and stays away from sugary sodas. Because he's so strict, some younger players have tried to copy him, hoping they can match his longevity and performance levels. Nutrition remains a key factor in his ongoing success.

69
THE "TONY HAWK" CONNECTION

Interestingly, Ronaldo once drew inspiration from skateboard legend Tony Hawk. He admired how Hawk transformed skateboarding through discipline, showmanship, and iconic tricks. Ronaldo felt that same mindset could apply to football: being bold, inventing new moves, and entertaining fans. Although skateboarding and soccer are quite different, the passion and drive to become the best have similarities. This unlikely influence shows how Ronaldo keeps an open mind, looking beyond football for ideas on self-improvement. He believes that greatness in any sport can teach lessons about hard work and creativity.

70
GOAL CELEBRATIONS WITH HIS SON

From time to time, Cristiano Jr. joins Ronaldo on the pitch after matches, especially when big victories occur. They've celebrated titles side by side, with Junior mimicking his father's famous "Siiii" jump. Such moments delight fans, revealing Ronaldo's playful, family-oriented side. It also inspires younger viewers, who see a global icon sharing triumphs with his child. These on-field celebrations demonstrate how he wants his family intimately involved in his career highlights. The bond between father and son sparks warm reactions and reminds everyone that even superstars cherish family closeness.

71
PUSKÁS AWARD
RECOGNITION

Although Ronaldo won the inaugural FIFA Puskás Award in 2009 for his incredible goal against Porto, he has been a finalist multiple times since then. The award honors the best goal scored worldwide each year. Some of his long-range screamers, bicycle kicks, and solo efforts have earned nominations. Even when he doesn't win, fans enjoy watching highlight reels of his top strikes. This shows how consistently he produces memorable moments. His repeated presence among finalists underscores that dramatic, top-quality finishes are a hallmark of his playing style.

72
"MY SON'S HERO IS MESSI"

Ronaldo once revealed in an interview that Cristiano Jr. actually admires Lionel Messi. While some fans found it surprising, Ronaldo wasn't upset. He laughed and said it's normal for kids to look up to great players, regardless of rivalries. This lighthearted moment showcased Ronaldo's confidence in himself and respect for Messi. It also highlighted that football, for many children, goes beyond club loyalties or individual rivalries. For Cristiano Jr., appreciating another star player simply reflects the love of the game that his father shares

73
FRIENDSHIP WITH PEPE

Ronaldo's bond with Portuguese defender Pepe is well-known. They've played together at Real Madrid and on the national team. Though their personalities differ—Pepe is more subdued while Ronaldo is outgoing—they mesh well on the pitch. Pepe acts as a protective force in defense, while Ronaldo leads the attack. Off the field, they share jokes, meals, and supportive words before big matches. In interviews, Pepe has praised Ronaldo's unwavering dedication, and Ronaldo has called Pepe a loyal friend who always has his back. Their longstanding friendship reflects mutual respect and trust.

74
CR7 FITNESS APP

In his quest to help others reach their fitness goals, Ronaldo launched the "CR7 Fitness" mobile app. It provides workout routines, diet tips, and motivational messages inspired by Ronaldo's training principles. Users can follow specialized programs focusing on core strength, cardio, or flexibility, each reflecting methods Ronaldo uses daily. Some routines even show short videos of him demonstrating exercises. He believes that sharing his secrets can inspire fans to lead healthier lives. The app's interactive features encourage people to track progress, turning personal fitness into a shared, motivational challenge.

75
HOMETOWN HOSPITAL PROJECT

Ronaldo once donated a significant sum to help build a pediatric hospital in Funchal, Madeira. This initiative aimed to provide better healthcare facilities for local children. He's grateful for his roots and wants to ensure the next generation can access quality medical care. Critics who say Ronaldo cares only about fame often change their minds when they learn of his hometown contributions. The hospital project embodies his determination to uplift his community, reflecting a belief that true success lies in giving back to those less fortunate.

76
A LOVE FOR TABLE TENNIS

Surprisingly, Ronaldo enjoys a good match of table tennis. Teammates recall how he used to challenge them in Manchester United's training ground recreation room. Skilled with fast reflexes, he sometimes outplayed the group, laughing when they tried to beat him. Table tennis helps keep his hand-eye coordination sharp, transferring those skills to quick footwork on the pitch. It's also a social sport that fosters camaraderie. Even after leaving United, he's been known to set up table tennis challenges at home or in hotels, proving that sports fun extends beyond football.

77
FIERCE FIFA COMPETITOR

Like many modern footballers, Ronaldo occasionally plays the FIFA video game series. Friends and teammates have shared that he's extremely competitive even in virtual matches, often demanding rematches if he loses. He enjoys playing as himself, controlling CR7 on the digital pitch to recreate his real-life moves. This playful hobby highlights Ronaldo's unwavering drive to win, no matter the setting. Kids worldwide can relate to his love of gaming, realizing that even the biggest superstars enjoy winding down with a controller, celebrating goals both on the screen and in stadiums.

78
An Instagram King

Ronaldo has the distinction of being one of the most-followed individuals on Instagram, boasting hundreds of millions of followers. He regularly posts updates about training, matches, family moments, and sponsorships. His account exemplifies how players can connect with fans, sharing glimpses of daily life and thoughts. Major brands also collaborate with him for product promotions. This massive reach reflects his global popularity, as people from diverse backgrounds admire his accomplishments. By leveraging social media positively, he inspires aspiring athletes and demonstrates that personal branding can thrive alongside athletic excellence.

79
SWIMMING AND WATER RELAXATION

After intense matches or training sessions, Ronaldo sometimes unwinds by swimming. He finds water therapy beneficial for relaxing tired muscles and reducing stress. In some clubs, he's requested facilities with swimming pools or hydrotherapy equipment for post-game recovery. His love for water-based exercises highlights a holistic approach to fitness. Beyond the physical benefits, swimming also offers mental peace, allowing him to clear his mind. He's been photographed at beach resorts enjoying a quick swim, proving that a splash in the pool can be as vital as any gym workout for rejuvenation.

80
MAINTAINING A SHREDDED PHYSIQUE

Ronaldo's body-fat percentage has been consistently reported to hover around or below 10%, incredibly low for a footballer. This level of leanness, combined with his muscular build, helps him accelerate faster and jump higher. Maintaining it requires intense cardio sessions, strict meal plans, and disciplined rest. Sports scientists have described him as having the physical condition of a top sprinter or gymnast. His dedication to staying lean demonstrates how crucial body composition can be for peak performance. Despite being in his 40s, he remains one of the fittest players on the planet.

81
MULTIPLE TIME
UCL TOP SCORER

Ronaldo has finished as the UEFA Champions League top scorer multiple times, underlining his remarkable consistency. Whether at Manchester United or Real Madrid, he's repeatedly dominated the competition's scoring charts. From close-range tap-ins to 30-yard rockets, his goals come in all forms. This success also reflects his strong mentality, as high-pressure matches often bring out his best. Teammates trust him to deliver in knockout stages, and he rarely disappoints. Many fans call the Champions League "Ronaldo's playground," a nod to how he elevates his game on Europe's grandest stage.

82
GOAL CELEBRATION HYBRIDS

Over the years, Ronaldo has experimented with different ways to celebrate goals. While the "Siiii" remains his most famous, he's sometimes combined it with a knee slide or pointed skyward in tribute to family members. He takes joy in mixing it up for big occasions or finals. Social media bursts with excitement whenever he debuts a new celebration, as fans try to copy it on local pitches. This playful side of his personality shines through, reminding everyone that scoring a goal is not just about the numbers—it's also about savoring the moment.

83
CO-AUTHORING
A KIDS' BOOK

Ronaldo once participated in a project that involved creating a children's story highlighting teamwork and perseverance. While he wasn't the main writer, his contributions focused on inspiring children to dream big. He provided anecdotes from his childhood, showing how practice and belief carried him forward. Although the book wasn't as widely publicized as his on-field successes, those who read it found a powerful message: that kindness, dedication, and a willingness to learn can take you far. This modest foray into literature underlines Ronaldo's desire to impact young audiences positively.

84
RONALDO
ROBO-MUSEUM

At the CR7 Museum in Madeira, there's a life-like robot figure of Ronaldo greeting visitors. Equipped with audio and sometimes responding to certain gestures, it's a futuristic attraction that surprises tourists. Kids find it both cool and a bit eerie, as the robot's expressions mimic Ronaldo's. The interactive display shares famous quotes, career stats, and interesting facts about him. This creative exhibit reflects Ronaldo's forward-thinking mindset, combining technology with storytelling to celebrate his journey. Visitors leave with memorable photos, feeling like they've met a sci-fi version of the football icon.

85
AVID TENNIS SPECTATOR

While football dominates his life, Ronaldo occasionally attends major tennis tournaments like the Madrid Open. He enjoys watching stars such as Rafael Nadal and Roger Federer, praising their skill and sportsmanship. By observing tennis athletes, he says he picks up mental strategies and learns about discipline, as top tennis players focus intensely on every single point. He appreciates how tennis demands endurance, precision, and a winning mindset—qualities similar to what he values in football. These visits to tennis events remind people that respect for other sports can broaden a player's horizons.

86
2008 ANKLE SURGERY

In 2008, Ronaldo had to face something that would worry any athlete—an ankle injury that needed surgery. Ouch! He had been playing so well for Manchester United, scoring goals left and right, when doctors told him he needed an operation to fix the problem. For a while, he had to stay off the pitch and focus on recovering through rehab, stretching, and special training. It was like a superhero getting his high-tech boots repaired before jumping back into action. And just like a superhero, Ronaldo didn't let the injury stop him—he came back even faster, stronger, and more determined than ever.

87
RESPECTFUL OF CLUB TRADITIONS

No matter which club Ronaldo has played for—Manchester United, Real Madrid, Juventus, or Al Nassr—he makes an effort to learn about its culture and traditions. He respects the legends who came before him, from Sir Bobby Charlton at United to Alfredo Di Stéfano at Real Madrid. This attitude endears him to long-time supporters who see him honoring their history. He often attends club anniversary events, meets older players, and pays homage to retired jersey numbers. His respect for tradition helps him fit in quickly and earn fans' admiration wherever he goes.

88
A MASTER AT PENALTIES

Ronaldo's penalty-taking technique involves a calm approach, a short run-up, and then an explosive strike. He's scored countless penalties under extreme pressure, whether in Champions League finals or international tournaments. While some players dislike the nerve-racking moment, Ronaldo thrives on the responsibility. He practices relentlessly, studying goalkeepers' tendencies and changing his run-up speed to keep them guessing. Even if he occasionally misses, his overall conversion rate is exceptionally high. This mastery from the spot has often saved his teams in crucial matches, further cementing his status as a go-to scorer.

89
ROLE MODEL FOR TEAMMATES

At clubs and with the national team, younger players look up to Ronaldo for guidance. They watch his training routines, see how he fuels his body, and try to replicate his commitment. Ronaldo offers tips on improving first touch, movement off the ball, and mental toughness. Coaches appreciate how he pushes teammates to match his standard in the gym and on the pitch. Although some might find his expectations daunting, most view his drive as a source of motivation. Through his example, a culture of excellence becomes the norm, raising overall team performance.

90
HIS UNIQUE FITNESS TEST

Ronaldo occasionally challenges himself with a fitness test called the yo-yo endurance test, which measures a player's ability to sprint back and forth between markers at increasing speeds, with minimal rest. He aims to outlast everyone else, treating it like a personal competition. Club fitness trainers have expressed amazement that he can still post top numbers, matching or even beating younger teammates. This test is part of why he maintains his form despite aging. It shows his relentless ambition to stay physically superior, refusing to let time slow him down.

91
BEARD OR CLEAN-SHAVEN?

Fans have noticed that Ronaldo sometimes experiments with facial hair—a small goatee during major tournaments or a stylish beard for magazine shoots. However, he tends to revert to a clean-shaven look for matches, citing comfort and brand consistency. He's joked that a beard can make him feel older, and he prefers a youthful, aerodynamic feel on the pitch. Although it might seem minor, Ronaldo's attention to appearance reflects his overall desire to present himself in a polished manner, both personally and for sponsors who value his iconic image.

92
MULTIPLE GOLDEN SHOES

The European Golden Shoe is awarded to the top scorer across all European leagues each season, adjusted for league difficulty. Ronaldo has won this award multiple times, reflecting his consistency in front of goal. He's captured it in the Premier League and La Liga, displaying that he can dominate scoring in different countries. Each time he earned the Golden Shoe, he dedicated it to fans and teammates, acknowledging football is a collective effort. These accolades also fed his hunger to keep breaking records, as he competes not only with opponents but with himself.

93
RELAXING ON YACHTS

When the season ends and it's time to unwind, Ronaldo often escapes to the sea on a yacht. Photographs show him basking in the sun, sometimes with family or close friends, away from the constant spotlight of training grounds. Sailing offers him tranquility and a chance to recharge mentally. He sometimes brings personal fitness gear onboard to maintain conditioning while on vacation. Whether anchored off the coast of Ibiza or cruising around Greek islands, this maritime break is key to keeping his mind fresh before the next intense season begins.

94
DOCUMENTARY
APPEARANCES

Ronaldo has starred in documentary projects that detail his life, training, and family moments. The 2015 film "Ronaldo" gave fans a behind-the-scenes view of his daily routine, how he juggles fame, and his role as a father. Such documentaries showcased his softer side, revealing the emotional bond he shares with his mother, siblings, and children. Viewers saw his intense practice sessions, the pressure of football, and the balance he seeks in everyday life. These films are popular with kids who admire him, as they discover a real person behind the football superstar.

95
INTERNATIONAL HAT-TRICKS

Ronaldo is famous for scoring hat-tricks not just in club football but also for Portugal. He's netted multiple hat-tricks in international matches, a testament to his continued brilliance whenever he puts on the national team jersey. Each hat-trick cements his legacy as the country's go-to goal-getter, carrying them through qualifying matches and tournaments. Portuguese fans see him as a hero who lifts the entire squad's morale. Young players dream of emulating these multi-goal performances, motivated by the idea that with hard work, they too could become game-changers for their country.

96
A STATUE ON MADEIRA

Outside the CR7 Museum stands a bronze statue of Ronaldo, unveiled in 2014. Crafted by a local sculptor, it showcases him in a classic pose, hands on hips, facing the ocean. Madeira's residents view the statue as a proud reminder that one of the world's greatest footballers hails from their island. Although some fans have teased the statue's facial expression, it remains a popular tourist spot for photos. Ronaldo has expressed gratitude for the tribute, saying it's humbling to have a permanent symbol of his achievements in his beloved hometown.

97
HAIRDRESSER
PARTNERSHIP

Ronaldo once partnered with a renowned hairdresser to create a series of CR7 haircare products. He stated that looking presentable is part of his self-confidence on the pitch. The line features styling gels, shampoos, and grooming tools, promoting a polished image for fans. While some see it as just another marketing move, Ronaldo believes grooming has an impact on self-esteem and performance. Kids who admire him might try these products, imagining they can replicate his stylish looks. This venture shows how he links athletic excellence with fashion and personal care.

98
"TOO MANY TROPHIES"

Over his career, Ronaldo has amassed well over 30 major trophies, including league titles, cups, and international honors. From multiple Champions Leagues to European Championship glory, his trophy cabinet overflows. He once joked that he had to build extra shelves to display everything. Each triumph symbolizes countless hours of training, diet control, and mental toughness. Collectively, they paint a picture of a man who refuses to rest on past success, always aiming to fill one more spot in his personal museum. That hunger sets him apart from many talented players.

99
KEYS TO LISBON

In 2016, Cristiano Ronaldo received a very special honour from the city of Lisbon—he was given the "keys to the city"! Now, this wasn't an actual key to open buildings, but a symbolic one, kind of like a magical golden key that says, "We're proud of you, and you'll always be welcome here." The mayor gave it to him as a way of showing respect and admiration for everything Ronaldo had achieved. Lisbon is extra special to Ronaldo because it's where his big football adventure truly began—he trained, played, and rose to fame there as a teenager with Sporting CP.

100
AMBITIONS BEYOND
RETIREMENT

Ronaldo has hinted he might explore coaching, management, or even club ownership after hanging up his boots. He's invested in multiple businesses, from hospitality to digital apps, showing a keen sense for enterprise. Some fans believe he could excel as a manager due to his leadership qualities and deep tactical understanding. Others think he might continue building the CR7 brand, expanding hotels, gyms, or fashion lines. Regardless, it's clear Ronaldo isn't one to sit idle. He'll channel his drive into new challenges, ensuring his influence on football and the broader world endures.

101
A LEGACY OF INSPIRATION

Perhaps Ronaldo's greatest achievement is inspiring millions of kids worldwide to chase their dreams. He rose from humble beginnings to global superstardom through grit, discipline, and unwavering belief. Countless young athletes idolize his dedication, trying to mimic his training routines or signature moves. Schools and community centers often feature his story as a lesson in perseverance. By continuing to break records and challenge himself in different leagues, Ronaldo shows that age and origin needn't limit success. Above all, his journey stands as proof that passion, hard work, and respect can create a true legend.

RONALDO TRIVIA

1. Where was Cristiano Ronaldo born?
A. Lisbon, Portugal
B. Funchal, Madeira (Portugal)
C. Porto, Portugal
D. Madrid, Spain

2. What is Cristiano Ronaldo's full name?
A. Cristiano André Ramos Ronaldo
B. Cristiano José De Santos Ronaldo
C. Cristiano Ronaldo dos Santos Aveiro
D. Cristiano Ronaldo Aveiro da Silva

3. Which local club did Ronaldo first play for as a child?
A. Marítimo
B. Sporting Braga
C. Porto Santo
D. Andorinha

4. At what age did Ronaldo move to Sporting Lisbon's youth academy?
A. 10
B. 12
C. 14
D. 16

5. What inspired Ronaldo's middle name, "Ronaldo"?
A. A famous Portuguese explorer
B. His father's favorite actor
C. Former U.S. President Ronald Reagan
D. A legendary Brazilian footballer

6. Against which team did a teenage Ronaldo impress Sir Alex Ferguson, leading to his transfer to Manchester United?
A. Benfica
B. Porto
C. Sporting Lisbon
D. Boavista

7. In which year did Ronaldo join Manchester United?
A. 2001
B. 2003
C. 2005
D. 2007

8. Which iconic jersey number did Sir Alex Ferguson insist Ronaldo wear at Manchester United?
A. 9
B. 10
C. 11
D. 7

9. How many Premier League titles did Ronaldo win during his first stint at Manchester United?
A. 1
B. 2
C. 3
D. 4

10. In what year did Ronaldo win his first Ballon d'Or?
A. 2005
B. 2008
C. 2009
D. 2010

11. Which club did Ronaldo join in 2009 for a then-world-record transfer fee of £80 million?
A. FC Barcelona
B. Juventus
C. Real Madrid
D. AC Milan

12. What is the name of Ronaldo's trademark goal celebration, involving a leap and a shout?
A. "Golazo!"
B. "Siiii!"
C. "Vamos!"
D. "Viva!"

13. In which UCL final did Ronaldo score a crucial penalty in the shootout, helping Manchester United win the trophy?
A. 2005 Final vs. AC Milan
B. 2008 Final vs. Chelsea
C. 2011 Final vs. Barcelona
D. 2012 Final vs. Bayern Munich

14. What was Ronaldo's jersey number when he first arrived at Real Madrid?
A. 7
B. 9
C. 10
D. 11

15. Which competition did Ronaldo and Real Madrid win four times during his stay at the club?
A. La Liga
B. Copa del Rey
C. UEFA Champions League
D. Spanish Super Cup

16. Which move is often referred to as the "Ronaldo Chop"?
A. A swift pass behind his standing leg
B. A trick where he spins in place
C. A two-footed jump over the ball
D. A sudden, high-speed step-over routine

17. In what year did Ronaldo help Portugal win the European Championship (UEFA Euro)?
A. 2008
B. 2012
C. 2016
D. 2021

18. Which of these was a reason Ronaldo left Sporting Lisbon early?
A. Homesickness for Madeira
B. Lack of playing time
C. Talent scouts signing him for Manchester United
D. A serious injury forced him to move clubs

19. Ronaldo first captained the Portuguese national team at which age?
A. 19
B. 20
C. 22
D. 23

20. How many times has Ronaldo been named the Best FIFA Men's Player (formerly FIFA Ballon d'Or) as of 2023?
A. 2
B. 3
C. 4
D. 5

21. Which of these is one of Ronaldo's well-known nicknames or short-brand names?
A. CR7
B. C-Ron
C. Ronny10
D. AveiroStar

22. Which club did Ronaldo join in 2018 from Real Madrid?
A. Manchester City
B. PSG
C. Juventus
D. Inter Milan

23. What major milestone did Ronaldo reach in October 2019?
A. 500 career goals
B. 600 career goals
C. 700 career goals
D. 750 career goals

24. What is the name of Ronaldo's museum in his hometown of Funchal, Madeira?
A. Museu do Cristiano
B. CR7 Museum
C. Casa de Ronaldo
D. The Aveiro Heritage Center

25. Which of the following is NOT a known trait of Ronaldo's playing style?
A. Exceptional free-kick ability
B. Tremendous aerial prowess
C. Reluctance to shoot from distance
D. Rapid, powerful dribbling

26. In 2021, Ronaldo returned to which club after leaving Juventus?
A. Real Madrid
B. FC Porto
C. Manchester United
D. Sporting Lisbon

27. When did Ronaldo become the men's all-time top scorer in international football?
A. 2016
B. 2018
C. 2020
D. 2021

28. Which number did Ronaldo initially wear upon joining Real Madrid?
A. 7
B. 9
C. 17
D. 77

29. Ronaldo helped Portugal clinch their first major international trophy at Euro 2016 by defeating which team in the final?
A. Spain
B. Germany
C. France
D. Italy

30. Which move did Ronaldo famously master to score spectacular goals, such as his one against Juventus in the Champions League?
A. Bicycle kick
B. Rabona
C. Scorpion kick
D. Flick shot

31. Which CR7 partner brand is known for Ronaldo's clothing and fashion line?
A. Nike
B. Adidas
C. CR7 Lifestyle
D. R7 Apparel

32. Ronaldo's father named him "Ronaldo" after which famous figure?
A. Ronald Reagan
B. Ronaldo Nazário
C. Ronaldinho Gaúcho
D. Ronald Koeman

33. Which item of personal memorabilia was famously donated by Ronaldo for a charity auction?
A. His 2008 Ballon d'Or replica
B. His golden boot from Manchester United
C. His Real Madrid debut jersey
D. His Euro 2016 final armband

34. How many UEFA Champions League titles has Ronaldo won?
A. 3
B. 4
C. 5
D. 6

35. Which of these charitable acts is Ronaldo widely known for?
A. Funding a wildlife sanctuary
B. Donating blood regularly
C. Buying books for public libraries
D. Establishing a school for technology

36. How many children does Cristiano Ronaldo have?
A. 2
B. 3
C. 4
D. 5

37. Ronaldo's famous leap during headers is often compared to what sport's vertical jump?
A. High jump
B. Basketball
C. Volleyball
D. Hurdling

38. Which of these clubs has Ronaldo NOT played for?
A. Al Nassr
B. Manchester City
C. Juventus
D. Sporting Lisbon

39. What personal attribute does Ronaldo credit for his exceptional free-kick style?
A. Luck and superstition
B. A unique striking technique and relentless practice
C. Coaching from Ronaldinho
D. Studying ancient soccer manuals

40. At Euro 2004, Ronaldo made his first senior tournament appearance for Portugal. How old was he then?
A. 17
B. 19
C. 21
D. 23

41. What is Ronaldo's primary motivation, as he has stated in interviews?
A. Becoming the richest athlete ever
B. Proving critics wrong
C. Being recognized as the best in history
D. Beating his own personal records each season

42. Which Major international trophy did Ronaldo finally win with Portugal in 2016?
A. FIFA World Cup
B. UEFA European Championship
C. Confederations Cup
D. Copa América

43. In 2022, Ronaldo made a high-profile move to which Saudi Arabian club?
A. Al Hilal
B. Al Ittihad
C. Al Nassr
D. Al Ahli

44. Which skill is Ronaldo known to have practiced by adding ankle weights during training?
A. Heading
B. Low passing
C. Penalty kicks
D. Slide tackling

45. Who is often referred to as Ronaldo's greatest rival in football history?
A. Zlatan Ibrahimović
B. Neymar Jr.
C. Lionel Messi
D. Wayne Rooney

46. Which personal brand did Ronaldo create, featuring clothing, fragrance, and lifestyle products?
A. CR7
B. Ron7
C. DosSantosStyle
D. AveiroX

47. Which youth club in Madeira did Ronaldo join at age 8?
A. Andorinha
B. Nacional
C. C.S. Marítimo
D. Funchal Academy

48. What is the name of the free-kick technique Ronaldo often uses that involves minimal spin and a dipping trajectory?
A. The Banana Kick
B. The Knuckleball
C. The Elastico
D. The Sidewinder

49. Against which team did Ronaldo score his famous overhead kick in the 2017–2018 Champions League quarterfinals?
A. Bayern Munich
B. FC Barcelona
C. Juventus
D. Atletico Madrid

50. Which of these best describes Ronaldo's goal celebration, known as the "Siiii"?
A. A salute to the crowd, followed by a backflip
B. A knee slide and pointing to the sky
C. A spin-jump followed by landing with arms down, shouting "Yes!"
D. Jumping over the corner flag in celebration

ANSWERS

1. (B) Funchal, Madeira (Portugal)
2. (C) Cristiano Ronaldo dos Santos Aveiro
3. (D) Andorinha
4. (B) 12
5. (C) Former U.S. President Ronald Reagan
6. (C) Sporting Lisbon
7. (B) 2003
8. (D) 7
9. (C) 3
10. (B) 2008
11. (C) Real Madrid
12. (B) "Siiii!"
13. (B) 2008 Final vs. Chelsea
14. (B) 9
15. (C) UEFA Champions League
16. (A) A swift pass behind his standing leg (the "Ronaldo Chop")
17. (C) 2016
18. (C) Talent scouts signing him for Manchester United
19. (D) 23
20. (D) 5
21. (A) CR7
22. (C) Juventus

23. (C) 700 career goals
24. (B) CR7 Museum
25. (C) Reluctance to shoot from distance (this is NOT a known trait; he loves shooting from distance)
26. (C) Manchester United
27. (D) 2021
28. (B) 9
29. (C) France
30. (A) Bicycle kick
31. (C) CR7 Lifestyle
32. (A) Ronald Reagan
33. (A) His 2008 Ballon d'Or replica
34. (C) 5
35. (B) Donating blood regularly
36. (D) 5
37. (B) Basketball
38. (B) Manchester City
39. (B) A unique striking technique and relentless practice
40. (B) 19
41. (D) Beating his own personal records each season
42. (B) UEFA European Championship
43. (C) Al Nassr
44. (A) Heading
45. (C) Lionel Messi
46. (A) CR7
47. (A) Andorinha
48. (B) The Knuckleball
49. (C) Juventus
50. (C) A spin-jump followed by landing with arms down, shouting "Yes!"

RONALDO QUOTES

1. "Talent without working hard is nothing."
Ronaldo stresses that even though having a natural gift for football can help, it's consistent effort and practice that truly drive success.

2. "I don't mind people hating me, because it pushes me."
In interviews, Ronaldo has acknowledged that criticism and negative opinions fuel his determination.

3. "We don't want to tell our dreams. We want to show them."
Here, Ronaldo highlights the importance of actions over words. Instead of simply talking about ambitions, he believes in demonstrating commitment and results on the pitch.

4. "I'm living a dream I never want to wake up from."
Reflecting on his journey from humble beginnings in Madeira to global stardom, Ronaldo shares his gratitude for his achievements.

5. "If you don't believe you are the best, then you will never achieve all that you are capable of."
Ronaldo values self-confidence as a cornerstone of success.

6. "Your love makes me strong, your hate makes me unstoppable."
In numerous social media posts and interviews, Ronaldo has acknowledged both the support of fans and the criticism from skeptics.

7. "Without football, my life is worth nothing."
Ronaldo's passion for the sport is clear in many interviews. This quote comes from his reflections on how football shaped his identity from childhood.

8. "I prefer other people to make judgments about the way I play and to characterize me, rather me describe myself."
Modesty isn't always associated with Ronaldo, but here he shows humility by suggesting that performances on the pitch should speak louder than self-praise.

9. "I see football as an art and all players are artists. If you are a top artist, the last thing you would do is paint a picture somebody else has already painted."
With this view, Ronaldo compares football to artistic creativity. He underscores individuality and innovation, advising players to develop their own style rather than copying others.

10. "I've never tried to hide the fact that it is my intention to become the best."
Ronaldo is frank about his ambition.

11. "If we can't help our family, who are we going to help?"
He has often spoken about the importance of supporting those close to him, especially given his humble background.

12. "If you think you're perfect already, then you never will be."
Similar to Messi's notion of constant improvement, Ronaldo highlights the danger of complacency.

13. "I still learn, but I think it's the best thing in life to have a kid."
In various interviews about fatherhood, Ronaldo speaks glowingly of his children.

14. "Scoring goals is a great feeling, but the most important thing to me is that the team is successful."
Although Ronaldo has a reputation for setting individual records, he reminds fans that teamwork and collective success matter greatly.

15. "Dedication, hard work all the time, and belief—this is the secret of success."
Ronaldo often credits these three factors for his longevity and record-breaking statistics.

QUOTES ON RONALDO

1. Lionel Messi on Ronaldo:
"Cristiano is an outstanding player with amazing qualities. We've shared the stage for many years, and I respect everything he's achieved in the game."

2. Sir Alex Ferguson on Ronaldo:
"Cristiano's work ethic and determination are second to none. He was the most gifted player I ever managed and a true professional on and off the pitch."

3. Zinédine Zidane on Ronaldo:
"For me, Cristiano is simply the best. He shows up in every match, scores goals, and leads by example. Coaching him was an absolute privilege."

4. José Mourinho on Ronaldo:
"Ronaldo is a player who makes the impossible look easy. His focus on continuous improvement is what sets him apart from everyone else."

5. Wayne Rooney on Ronaldo:
"I saw firsthand how he pushed himself in training every day. He constantly aimed to be the best. We became good friends, and I learned so much from his mindset."

6. Carlo Ancelotti on Ronaldo:
"Cristiano is the ultimate professional, always putting in extra hours. He never stops wanting to improve, even after winning everything."

7. Pelé on Ronaldo:
"I admire his ability to always be decisive in the big moments. Cristiano is someone who has earned respect through discipline and a lot of hard work."

8. Gary Neville on Ronaldo:
"He turned up at Manchester United as a talented kid and left as the world's best player. His dedication was unlike anything I'd seen before."

9. David Beckham on Ronaldo:
"Cristiano's passion for the game is clear every time he steps on the pitch. He has delivered at every level and continues to raise the bar."

10. Rio Ferdinand on Ronaldo:
"When I look back at his training habits, it's no surprise he became such a phenomenon. He drove himself to levels we didn't think were possible."

11. Raúl González on Ronaldo:
"Cristiano brought a winning mentality to Real Madrid. He believed every match could be won, and he inspired that in the entire squad."

12. Kylian Mbappé on Ronaldo:
"Cristiano is a hero of mine. If you're a young player and you love football, you love Cristiano Ronaldo."

13. Zlatan Ibrahimović on Ronaldo:
"Cristiano is a machine. He works very hard and has played at the top level for many years. You can only respect that."

14. Luka Modrić on Ronaldo:
"Cristiano was always pushing us to be better. He led by example. Training with him meant you always had to be at your best."

15. Novak Djokovic on Ronaldo:
"I admire Cristiano Ronaldo. He is a great athlete and a great example of how someone can build up their body and mindset to be the best."

FULL TIME!

Wow, what an incredible journey we've had learning about Cristiano Ronaldo! From his unstoppable goal-scoring to his tireless work ethic and dedication to charity, we've uncovered so many fun and fascinating facts about his life. Ronaldo's story shows us that with passion, hard work, and fearless ambition, we can achieve extraordinary things.

We've seen how Ronaldo broke countless records, led his teams to victory time after time, and inspired young players around the world to follow their dreams. We've learned about his close bond with family, his impressive car collection, and his commitment to causes like health care and children's charities. Every fact reveals a new side of Ronaldo, making him even more inspiring.

We've left the next few pages blank so you can write down and journal what your biggest lessons from Lionel Messi are. Use this space to reflect on how Messi's journey inspires you and what dreams you want to achieve.

Thank you for joining us on this adventure through the life of Cristiano Ronaldo. We hope you've enjoyed discovering all these amazing facts. Now, go out there and make your own magic, just like Ronaldo!

WHAT HAVE YOU LEARNED FROM RON?

Printed in Dunstable, United Kingdom